Zion National Park Tour Guide Book

By Waypoint Tours

Front Cover - Angels Landing Rising Above the Virgin River

Back Cover - Zion Canyon View from Emerald Pools Trail

WAYPOINT TOURS®

Zion National Park Waypoint Tour®

Contents

Tour Maps	Page 4
1) Zion	Page 6
2) Zion Canyon Visitor Center	Page 8
3) Pa'rus Trail	Page 10
4) Watchman Trail	Page 12
5) Zion Museum	Page 14
6) Zion-Mount Carmel Highway	Page 16
7) Canyon Overlook Trail	Page 18
8) Court of the Patriarchs	Page 20
9) Zion Lodge	Page 22
10) Emerald Pools Trails	Page 24
11) The Grotto & Angels Landing Trail	Page 26
12) Hidden Canyon & Weeping Rock Trails	Page 30
13) Temple of Sinawava & Riverside Walk	Page 34
14) The Narrows	Page 36
15) Kolob Canyons	Page 38
16) Bryce Canyon	Page 40
17) Grand Canyon South Rim	Page 42
18) Grand Canyon North Rim	Page 44
Tour Maps	Page 46
Optional CD & DVD Info	Page 49
Notes	Page 50

Gas station
Exit 42

To Cedar City,
Cedar Breaks National Monument,
and Salt Lake City

North

WAYPOINT TOURS®

**Zion Tour
Kolob Canyons Area**

Horse Ranch Mountain
8726ft
2659m

Exit 40

Kolob Canyons Road

PARIA

Taylor Creek Trail

North Fork

Middle Fork

Double Arch Alcove

South Fork

Lee Pass Trailhead

15

**Kolob Canyons
Viewpoint**

**Kolob Canyons
Visitor Center**

5074ft
1546m

Timber Creek
Overlook Trail

K O L O B

C A N Y O N S

Nagunt Mesa
7785ft
2372m

La Verkin Creek Trail

Willis Creek

BEAR TRAP CANYON

Chasm Lake

8055ft
2455m

TIMBER TOP MOUNTAIN

Gregory Butte
7705ft
2348m

**Kolob
Arch**

Kolob Arch Trail

Langston Mountain
7408ft
2258m

Beatty Spring

La Verkin Creek

Timber Creek

Hop Valley Trail

HOP VALLEY

LONG POINT

Burnt Mountain
7682ft
2341m

C L I F F S

H U R R I C A N E

La Verkin Creek

1) Zion*
2) Visitor Center
3) Pa'rus Trail
4) Watchman Trail*
5) Zion Museum
6) Zion-Mount Carmel Highway*
7) Canyon Overlook Trail*
8) Court of the Patriarchs
9) Zion Lodge
10) Emerald Pools Trails*
11) The Grotto & Angels Landing Trail*
12) Weeping Rock & Hidden Canyon Trails*
13) Temple of Sinawava & Riverside Walk*
14) The Narrows
15) Kolob Canyons*

LOWER

Beyond this point, road
not plowed in winter

Firepit Knoll
7265ft
2214m

**Hop Valley
Trailhead**

Connector Trail

KOLOB

Spendlove Knoll
6895ft
2102m

LEE VALLEY

SMITH MESA

PLATEAU

Kolob Terrace Road

Tabernacle Dome
6430ft
1960m

Unpaved roads are
impassable when wet

**Left
Fork
Trail
head**

4

Zion Tour

WAYPOINT TOURS®

1) Zion*
2) Visitor Center
3) Pa'rus Trail
4) Watchman Trail*
5) Zion Museum
6) Zion-Mount Carmel Highway*
7) Canyon Overlook Trail*
8) Court of the Patriarchs
9) Zion Lodge
10) Emerald Pools Trails*
11) The Grotto & Angels Landing Trail*
12) Weeping Rock & Hidden Canyon Trails*
13) Temple of Sinawava & Riverside Walk*
14) The Narrows
15) Kolob Canyons*

North ↑

West Rim Trail

THE NARROWS

ORDERVILLE CANYON

Mountain of Mystery
6565ft
2001m

East Mesa Trail

Cabin Spring

7367ft
2245m

West Rim Trail

Riverside Walk

14

13 Temple of Sinawava

Weeping Rock

ECHO CANYON

12

Hidden Canyon Trail

HEAPS CANYON

CANYON

Angels Landing

The Great White Throne
6744ft 2056m

11

10

Emerald Pools Trails

The Grotto

COURT OF THE PATRIARCHS

9 **Zion Lodge**

ZION NATIONAL PARK

ZION

8

Zion Canyon Scenic Drive

Spring through fall, Zion Canyon Scenic Drive is open to shuttle buses only. Private vehicles are not allowed beyond Canyon Junction.

The Sentinel
7157ft
2181m.

TOWERS OF THE VIRGIN

Altar of Sacrifice
7505ft
2288m

The East Temple
7709ft 2350m

Canyon Junction

1

Canyon Overlook Trail

7

Tunnel

Zion Human History Museum

The West Temple
7810ft
2380m

5

Parus Trail

6 Zion-Mount Carmel Highway

Tunnel
No bikes or pedestrians allowed. Ask about restrictions on large vehicles.

3

South Entrance

1

2

4 Watchman Trail

Zion Canyon Visitor Center

Springdale
3920ft
1195m

Mount Kinesava
7285ft
2220m

9

North Fork Virgin River

The Watchman 6545ft 1995m

www.waypointtours.com

1) Zion

Welcome to Zion, a land of sheer cliffs, ancient sand dunes, amazing vistas, and verdant garden alcoves.

How did Zion come to be named Zion? Pioneer Isaac Behunin, leafing through the Book of Isaiah one evening, was struck by the way the setting sun's last ruddy light hit Red Arch Mountain. The name came to him by epiphany as he skimmed through Isaiah chapter 2 verse 3: "And many people shall go and say, Come ye, and let us go up the mountain of the Lord … and we will walk in his paths: for out of Zion shall go forth the law."

Mormon pioneers believed that Zion meant "sanctuary" and its rugged beauty was proof that God wanted them to settle there. However, in the early 1900's, visiting photographers, artists, and a surveyor named Leo Snow argued that Zion was far too beautiful to keep secret from the rest of the world. In 1909, President Howard Taft elevated Zion to national monument status under the Paiute name Mukuntuweap, meaning "straight canyon." However, like the Paiute American Indians themselves, the name, which had existed here for over 800 years, was already fading from the region. In 1919, when the United States Congress upgraded Mukuntuweap from monument to national park status, they renamed it "Zion" at the urging of the new Utahans.

Now about 2.5 million pilgrims from around the world are drawn here each year. Some come to gaze in awe at the majesty of Zion's grandeur with pedestals of stone so tall and massive they seem to support the sky. Rock climbers pit their muscle against these mighty walls, inching upward on ascents that can last days. Geologists work in the opposite direction. Descending the walls and tracking changes in the rock, they can almost travel back through time, learning how our planet works by understanding the changes it has undergone. Others come to celebrate the diversity of life housed here. Reminiscent of Eden, Zion sustains an impressive species list of 800 plants, 75 mammals, 271 birds, 32 reptiles and amphibians, and 6 native fish.

Zion is also nirvana for the hiker. The park's trails offer a full spectrum of hiking challenges. Following these paths can mean anything from a leisurely riverside stroll, to a multi-night backpack, to a white-knuckled, chain-assisted ascent over 1000 feet above the ground.

Zion is also a crown jewel of the National Park Service, a shining result of the dedication of men and women who strive to leave these works of nature clean, beautiful, and natural, for the enjoyment of future generations. As you begin your own Zion experience, be prepared as you will soon understand exactly the grandeur that overcame Isaac Behunin when he named this place, Zion.

2) Zion Canyon Visitor Center

Built in 2000, the Zion Canyon Visitor Center is the gateway to the heart of the park. The building was carefully designed to be as environmentally friendly as possible. To that end, all of the exhibits are located outside. This not only provides enough space for everybody to efficiently plan their visit and learn more about the park's natural and cultural history, it also saves money and energy by not having to heat, cool, and clean a large, indoor exhibit hall.

One of the most popular exhibits is a 3-dimensional scaled model of Zion Canyon. The lessons learned here may save your life. Seeing the towering walls and narrow canyons in miniature should give you a better idea of how steep and challenging some of the hikes really are. To make the model even more educational and fun, use a couple of water bottles to simulate rain. See what kind of chaos is created in the canyons by merely sprinkling a couple cups of water on the model's cliff tops. Now imagine the full-scale destruction delivered by a multi-billion gallon thunderstorm. You might want to check the weather forecast!

Inside the visitor center, you can get up-to-date weather and hiking information from a helpful park ranger as well as peruse the Zion Natural History Association Bookstore.

The Zion Canyon Visitor Center is the main terminus for the Zion Canyon Shuttle. Unless you are staying at the Zion Lodge, the Zion Canyon Shuttle is the only way to gain access to the heart of Zion from April through October. Those who have visited Zion prior to the shuttle service often testify as to how much less crowded the inner canyon feels, and how much more wildlife can be seen from the now quieter roads. It is important that you also register your opinion. The National Park Service is looking for sustainable solutions that will continue to allow as many people as possible to love America's national parks … without accidentally loving them to death.

3) Pa'rus Trail

This trail offers a leisurely 3.5-mile round-trip riverside stroll, between the Zion Canyon Visitor Center and Canyon Junction. Pa'rus translates from Paiute as "bubbling tumbling stream." Renamed the Virgin River, this watercourse fuels the very life force of the park, and consequently makes this a good trek for spying wildlife. Another reason for this trail's popularity is that, unlike most national park trails, bicycles and dogs are permitted, providing you are mindful of the "rules of the road."

While the presence of pavement, dogs, and bicycles might be reminiscent of a city park, make no mistake, this is still a national park. Even on this trail, the chance still exists that you might have an encounter with one of Zion's two most shy, but infamous animals, the mountain lion and the Great Basin rattlesnake. While neither creature lives up to its wildly exaggerated reputation, both can be dangerous if not respected.

If you encounter a rattlesnake in the middle of the trail, it is usually safer for you to temporarily leave the trail than try to convince the snake to do so. A rattlesnake bite can be deadly, but usually only if you become hysterical or follow the antiquated advice of applying a tourniquet, cutting into the wound with a pocketknife, and sucking on the bite. Do not do that. Instead, leave the wound alone. If possible, send somebody for help. Otherwise, go for help on your own, avoiding unnecessary exertion, which can accelerate the slow spread of the venom through your body.

When mountain lions hunt, they prefer darkness, deer, deserted prey, and fear. You can protect yourself by hiking during the day, with other humans, and by behaving aggressively toward any mountain lion that is not already running the other way.

Some might argue that dangerous animals should be removed from national parks. Others might retort, "In that case, humans should be the first to go." The National Park Service's more moderate approach is to use education to protect the people from the wild animals, and rules and regulations to protect the animals from the wild people.

4) Watchman Trail

Across the road from the Zion Canyon Visitor Center shuttle stop, the moderate 2.7-mile Watchman Trail leads to the top of the low bluff overlooking the visitor center. Though not as famous as other Zion hikes, on this trail you can enjoy some peace and quiet, while soaking in the tranquil majesty of the setting sun.

After leaving the banks of the Virgin River, the Watchman Trail crosses the drier flats, where the green-grey sagebrush is punctuated with prickly pear cacti and other colorful desert flowers, such as trailing four o'clocks, paintbrushes, and marigolds. The trail soon enters a side canyon and climbs through the thin, dark red, cliff-forming Springdale sandstone. The trail ends in a small loop that showcases the grand panorama of Zion and the Watchman monolith that guards the entrance of Zion. Uplifting, faulting, lava flows, and rapid erosion are just a few of the features that make this region so geologically interesting and aesthetically pleasing.

Look for the Springdale sandstone on both sides of the canyon. By following these converging red lines, you can see how the rock layers are not flat, but actually slope downward into the upper portions of the canyon. This downward slope indicates that the lower Virgin River has and will continue to easily cut a wide channel through the older and softer siltstone and limestone, while the upper Virgin will long continue to struggle with the much harder and younger sandstones, and only slowly deepening Zion's famously narrow and vertical inner canyons.

While descending to the visitor center, you may notice that as the canyon widens, the number of dwellings increases correspondingly. People have been fascinated with the canyon since its discovery in 1858 by Levi Johnson, who was surveying the area for Brigham Young. Within 25 years, several families had homesteaded in the canyon, including the Crawfords near the Zion Museum, and the Heaps near the Zion Lodge. Flash flooding and reduced hours of direct sunlight make narrow canyons unappealing places to live, however. Long before Zion became a national park, humans realized that while the inner canyons are exciting places to explore, they are not necessarily the best places to live. Today's visitors can help preserve the beauty and natural wildlife of the canyons by staying on the maintained trails and "leaving no trace behind."

Top - Sunset View from Watchman Trail
Bottom - Canyon View from Watchman Trail

5) *Zion Museum*

At the Zion Human History Museum, located less than a mile north of the Zion Canyon Visitor Center, you can learn how water has shaped the geology, ecology and the pattern of human existence in Zion through the displays and orientation film. From the back patio, you can view the Temple and Towers of the Virgin. This famous panorama is best photographed in the early morning light.

To the north of the museum, you can look down into the main canyon across the fields once tended by William, Cornelia, and J.J. Crawford. See if you can spy the "bridge" near the top of Bridge Mountain from the shuttle stop. Because this impressive natural feature was not carved by flowing water, it is technically a natural arch. From this distance, it looks more like something made from a spider web filament rather than sandstone. In actuality, the span is nearly 80 feet long and 20 feet high.

The more common type of arch in Zion is the blind, or "almost" arch, which has not yet eroded enough to create an actual hole. In fact, there is no guarantee that a blind arch will continue to erode in precisely the right way to form a true arch. The entire primordial span could just as easily collapse, instead creating a smooth cliff wall, and starting the erosion process all over again. The Great Arch of Zion is a classic example of a blind arch.

Top - Crawford Arch Natural Bridge in Center
Bottom - Zion Museum

6) Zion-Mount Carmel Highway

As you travel along the busy Zion-Mount Carmel highway, it is hard to imagine a time when Zion's annual visitation was less than 10,000 people. While Zion has always been accessible from the west, water-filled slot canyons forced all but the most adventurous to return back east the way they came. Prior to the completion of this highway, the only other way through Zion was rancher John Winder's treacherous Echo Canyon Trail, which was so steep that horses and cows occasionally slipped from it, and fell to their deaths. The 24-mile long Zion-Mount Carmel Highway was opened July 4, 1930 after three years of work.

As you travel eastward, the first engineering feat you come to was actually the last one completed. The Pine Creek Bridge was designed by Harry Langley, who directed workers from a scale model he created by painstakingly carving every block from bars of soap. His meticulous design not only specified the exact shape of every stone, but also its color; each color representing a different layer of rock found within Zion.

As some of Zion's oldest rock layers were forming, dinosaurs trekked across the land, and ancient fish swam in the lakes. Nearby in the Moenave Formation, the scales of a fresh water fish called Semionotus, similar to modern day Sturgeon, were discovered. Dinosaur tracks have been found in the Kayenta mudstone and can be seen on the backcountry "Left Fork of North Creek" or "Subway" hikes. Other fossils, including starfish, petrified wood, and bison bones have been found in the many geologic layers of Zion. Keep your eyes open … but do not take any souvenirs!

The 5,613-foot long tunnel through Jurassic period Navajo sandstone was completed in 345 days and for half the cost of the 3.6 miles of switchbacks across the Kayenta sandstone slopes. The tunneling began by blasting galleries from which perpendicular tunnels were simultaneously drilled. The six galleries served to expedite the tunneling, and provide natural light and ventilation. Today you can glimpse breathtaking views through them, but only from a moving car – no stopping allowed!

Emerging from the tunnel, you enter a slick rock world of rolling, textured Navajo Sandstone buttes. The repeated pattern of curving lines found in these yellow-white rock mounds is called cross-bedding. They are individual cross-sections of sand dunes standing as testament to the vast desert that covered Utah 180 million years ago, a desert with sands deeper than the Sahara.

The most famous of these buttes is Checkerboard Mesa. In addition to the horizontal cross-bedding, this conical monolith also looks as if it was squeezed against the mesh of a gigantic fishing net. The erosion process that carved the vertical lines is not well understood, but it is thought to be influenced by cracking due to freezing and thawing.

Built for the once-controversial cost of $1.9 million, few now question the scenic value of the Zion-Mount Carmel Highway, which stretches from the Checkerboard Mesa to the tunnel and connects Zion to the wider world.

Top - Pine Creek Bridge
Bottom - Checkerboard Mesa

7) Canyon Overlook Trail

Trying to build up the nerve to hike the arduous Angels Landing trail? Perhaps you should warm up on the 1-mile round-trip Canyon Overlook Trail. The drop-offs along this trail are better protected by boardwalks, railings, and fences; and the views are very impressive, especially at sunrise.

After the initial scores of rough-hewn steps, the trail stays mainly level, but offers thrilling views down into the dark depths of the Pine Creek Slot Canyon. As with every trail in Zion, resist the urge to perform any gravity experiments. Park rangers have zero tolerance for rock throwers! Too many injuries have occurred when people were certain that "there couldn't be anybody down there!" Case in point, the Pine Creek Slots just below are a favorite among canyoneers. It is a technical slither requiring rope work for anybody who is not part lizard.

In actuality, it would be surprising to find a real lizard in the depths of Pine Creek, because much of the canyon never receives direct sunlight. Lizards, being exothermic, strive to maintain a perfect body temperature, so they are seldom more than a short sprint away from both full sun and cool shade. Look for the masters of speed, the plateau and western whiptail lizards with bright blue tails twice as long as their bodies.

The trail arrives at the canyon rim in a slick rock pocket, where the scenery before you demands your attention, while inviting your curiosity. As the sun rises and the shadows recede from these towering cliffs, can you guess what has caused the dramatic colored stains on the rocks silhouetted against the gradually lightening sky? The blood red stains on the higher white cliffs are left behind when rain dissolves the iron in the overlying Temple Cap Formation, which then seeps into and stains the rocks below.

The skinny, dark black stains are caused by rainstorms washing organic materials over the cliffs. Locals are often amused when visitors complain about the rain. Rainstorms are not only uncommon at Zion, they are also of short duration. However, anybody who has witnessed the 500 to 1000-foot waterfalls gushing out of the hanging canyons knows there can be no more memorable time to visit the park.

White stains are due to either salt precipitating out of solution near a spring line, or feces from cliff-nesting birds like common ravens, golden eagles, and peregrine falcons. Finally, there are the mysterious desert varnishes, which are the shiny dark purple to reddish-brown blotches that appear to have been splashed on the walls by some gigantic abstract painter. Desert varnish is thought to be formed by algae known as cyanobacteria. As part of their metabolic processes, these tiny creatures mix a minute amount of manganese and water. With hundreds living on a square inch of rock, it takes billions of them, living and dying over thousands of years, to create the larger stains.

While gazing at the rainbow of rocks, a railing with chain-link fence keeps you from going where only lizards would dare. Here, you are perched atop the Great Arch of Zion!

Top - Sunrise View from Canyon Overlook
Bottom - Great Arch of Zion below
Canyon Overlook

8) Court of the Patriarchs

Few people have left a more lasting legacy on such a famous landscape as Frederick Vining Fisher did for Zion. Fisher was a Methodist minister who, during a single day's visit to the park in 1916, bestowed six immortal names on the park's most famous landmarks.

Hop off the shuttle at the Court of the Patriarchs and hike the short but steep trail for an awesome view of Fisher's first trio: Abraham, Isaac, and Jacob from left to right. In front of Jacob is a smaller sandstone horn, which was later named Moroni, for the angel in Mormon theology who delivered the Book of Mormon as golden tablets to founder Joseph Smith. A few hours later, Fisher went on to name Angels Landing, the Pulpit, and the Great White Throne.

Christianity was not the first religion to leave its mark on the rocks of Zion. The Zion Canyon Scenic Drive ends in an immense citadel of stone called the Temple of Sinawava, the Paiute American Indian name for their wolf deity. Indeed, some archeologists surmise that some of the petroglyphs carved into Zion's walls by the earlier Fremont and Anasazi cultures are icons from their more ancient theology.

In some cases, Zion's names are more stable than the monoliths themselves. The Paiute blamed frequent rockfalls on their moody and treacherous deity, Kinesava. In the early 1880's, a huge slab crashed down, burying the farm of Mormon pioneer Oliver D. Gifford. The blind arch created in those horrifying seconds gave the peak its current name, Red Arch Mountain. The Gifford family miraculously escaped unscathed but they did decide to relocate to Springdale.

Looking down the canyon to your left, you will see the more persistent and notorious Sentinel Slide. Approximately 8,000 years ago, an entire sandstone fin similar to Angels Landing collapsed, filling the canyon with debris and damming the Virgin River, creating a lake 200 feet deep that extended up canyon to the Temple of Sinawava. It is unclear whether it took tens or hundreds of years for the river to free itself, or how many times in prehistory the slide re-dammed the river. In 1995, the Sentinel Slide slumped again, temporarily damming the river and stranding 300 visitors in the canyon. The National Park Service repaired the road, but any park ranger will tell you that the story is far from over. Zion could not be Zion without continuous rock falls and landslides.

Top - Three Patriarchs
Bottom - Sentinel Slide

9) Zion Lodge

Built in 1925 by the National Park Service and the Union Pacific Railroad, with lumber brought down from the upper cliffs by Flannigan's cable works, the Zion Lodge was the first night's stay on the famous 4-day "Grand Circle Tour." Visitors arrived by train in Cedar City, and were bused to Zion, the North Rim of the Grand Canyon, Bryce Canyon, and finally Cedar Breaks before returning to Cedar City. In 1968, the Zion Lodge burned to the ground. It was hastily rebuilt to be ready for the next tourist season, but unfortunately, not all of its original charm could be restored.

Nevertheless, the lodge is still the place to get a good meal with an incredible view, explore Zion by horseback, attend an informative evening program presented by a park ranger, or just relax on the lawn, soaking in the grandeur of the surroundings.

While relaxing in the rustic rocking chairs, or sprawling on the lawn beneath the big tree, you may notice a breeze that cools the canyon. In the early morning, the breeze flows into the canyon as the plains beyond the canyon heat up. At night, the flow reverses as the cool air from the upper mesas drops back down into the canyon. Interestingly, the flow, and therefore the cooling action, is most noticeable at the base of the canyon, making the lodge location ideal.

On this same sprawling lawn, you may encounter mule deer and wild turkey that also frequent the vicinity of the lodge. Please enjoy these animals from a safe distance. Ironically, those who mean these animals the least harm are sometimes the ones who harm them the most … by feeding them. True animal lovers realize that while feeding wild animals may be immediately gratifying, it will too often end in the premature demise of the animals. Over the long term, most human food is toxic to wild animals. While being fed, animals can also become dangerously bold and aggressive.

10) Emerald Pools Trails

A 2 to 3-mile hike to the Emerald Pools can begin or end at either the Zion Lodge or the Grotto Trailhead. Consult a park map to better understand your hiking options. No route is complete without the additional half-mile round trip spur from the middle pool to the upper pool. One of the most popular hikes in the park, the Emerald Pools Trails offer beautiful views, and while hiking in the twilight, you might see some of Zion's famous nocturnal animals.

Many of Zion's 19 species of bats love hunting in this canyon because the pools and vegetation attract a cornucopia of insects. Though noisy, the calls of frogs and toads are intentionally hard to trace back to their owners. While trying to pinpoint a frog's location, be careful not to trip over a porcupine. Protected by quills that can penetrate all but the thickest leather, these large rodents may try to bluff you into yielding the trail to them. Finally, look for ringtail cats. Occasionally mistaken for lemurs, these nimble tree and cliff-climbers are smaller than foxes, and have bushy, white and black tails that reveal their distant relation to raccoons.

The upper Emerald Pool is recharged by a waterfall that highlights the joints in the rock as it tumbles through them. If you are careful not to disturb the still waters of the middle pool, you may see thousands of tadpoles and a beautiful reflection of Red Arch Mountain, which peers into Heaps Canyon from the far side of the main canyon. Extra caution is necessary when crossing the usually wet and slippery expanse of slick rock beside the middle pool. Do not approach the brink. Although the fall is less than 60 feet and ends in a shallow pool of water, this fall has claimed more lives than any other in Zion.

The cool walk below the lower falls shows how water can rejuvenate and bring life to the canyon, and form new rocks. As the water begins to trickle or drip down the alcove, the minerals dissolved in it precipitate out. It forms a new rock called travertine, similar to cave stalactites and stalagmites.

11) The Grotto & Angels Landing Trail

The most famous of all Zion's hikes is Angels Landing that was dedicated in 1926 by the Prince and Princess of Sweden. It is not the most popular hike, however, and for good reason. This 1500-foot climb and 5-mile round trip hike is beyond the ability of some people's muscles, and other people's nerves. The final approach is an unprotected knife-back ridge with a 1200-foot drop on one side, and a 400-foot drop on the other. However, for those in good physical condition and without a fear of heights, this is a must-do hike.

Beginning across the river at the Grotto, which was a campground in the 1920's, the trail starts gradually with a leisurely riverside stroll beneath cottonwood trees that also date back to the 1920's. After the park was established, the cottonwood forest, formerly suppressed by farming, recovered. However, why aren't there any younger trees growing to replace older ones? In the 1930's, much of the Virgin River's channel was reinforced with stone-filled wire boxes called revetments. The CCC, Civilian Conservation Corps, and the National Park Service did this to minimize the destruction and mess created during seasonal flash flooding.

The revetments have worked so well, for so long, that the river seldom escapes its channel, and thus no longer floods the valley floor. Cottonwood seeds require flooded soil to germinate, and young cottonwood saplings must have their roots in water to grow. This is the key to the cottonwood forests' long-term survival, as well as all the other plants and animals that call these forests home.

The obvious answer of letting natural floods return is not popular with many park visitors, or the tourism industry that depends on them. Correcting ecological mistakes is never easy but as the trail approaches the "Big Bend" and the formation beneath Angels Landing known as the "Organ", you are approaching an area the National Park Service is letting return to a more natural state. Here, the river is allowed to meander more freely, and a cottonwood reforestation project has begun.

After conquering the steep climb into Refrigerator Canyon, you will be rewarded with a classic view of the Great White Throne. Both this mighty gleaming monolith and Angels Landing were named by Methodist minister Frederick Vining Fisher. You will soon see why Fisher, thinking only an angel could set foot on its summit, so named this destination.

In the back of Refrigerator Canyon, you will climb one of the most impressively engineered sets of switchbacks found anywhere. Called Walter's Wiggles, this portion of the trail was named for the park superintendent who oversaw its construction. At the top of Walter's Wiggles, you can size up the knife-back approach to the summit from amongst the pentamon, spiderwort, sand verbena, and other desert flowers blooming at Scout Lookout. Be assured that the most treacherous sections of the route are equipped with chains, for those who only feel comfortable advancing when they can have a death grip on something sturdy.

Upon reaching the summit, don't be too surprised if you suddenly see somebody pulling themselves up over the lip of the cliff. Angels Landing is also one of the many popular technical rock-climbing challenges Zion has to offer ... and you thought your route was difficult!

12) Hidden Canyon & Weeping Rock Trails

Hidden Canyon is a classic example of a hanging canyon, and offers several insights into the geologic forces that have shaped Zion National Park. With a much smaller watershed than that of the Virgin River, Hidden Canyon has been left behind high and relatively dry compared to the main Zion Canyon which is being deepened and widened by the fury of erosion. The hike to the mouth of Hidden Canyon is only a 2-mile round trip, but with an 850-foot climb, it is steeper than even the Angels Landing Trail. Like Angels Landing, the last portion of this trail has a section of high exposure, partially equipped with chains.

Before you start climbing, tilt your head back to locate the heavy beam structure perched on the very peak of Cable Mountain. This is the remnant of an early 1900's logging cabledraw works that lowered lumber from the forested mesas 2000 feet above to the valley floor below. This device was the brainchild of David Flannigan, who sought to fulfill a prophecy of Mormon Church President Brigham Young, who said upon visiting Zion Canyon in 1863, that timber would one day come down off the cliffs "like a hawk flies."

The trail takes you up to a series of "potholes" at the mouth of Hidden Canyon. "Potholes" form when gravel trapped in pocketed streams swirls around, grinding a hole deeper and deeper. If you continue your hike back into the canyon, you can see intricate honeycombs that formed when the calcium carbonate "cement" holding the sand grains together dissolved, and the grains are plucked one by one from the cliff faces by wind and rain. An up-close view of a blind arch can also be found back in the recesses of Hidden Canyon.

As you travel back down the trail to Weeping Springs, it is easy to observe how the differential weathering helps alcoves, arches and sheer cliffs form. High above and out of sight, water from summer rains and winter snows slowly percolates down through the Navajo sandstone, starting a long subterranean journey that eventually ends at the roof of an alcove 1000 feet below. Near the bottom of the Navajo sandstone lie thin beds of impermeable shale that prevent the water from moving any further downward. Instead, the percolating water saturates the sandstone at the shale bed contact and begins to move laterally. The water emerges from the canyon wall and the weaker rock erodes. The overhanging rock fractures along vertical joints and then falls away, forming sheer cliff faces. Since an arch is structurally the strongest geometry, the remaining overhanging rock is gradually shaped into an arch.

The Weeping Rock Trail is fun year-round, but especially refreshing on a hot summer day after hiking the Hidden Canyon Trail. As the name implies, this half-mile round trip stroll takes you to the base of a cliff where there is always water dripping. A spring line marks the plane where the pooled water finds its way out of the cliff. As you approach this sprinkling alcove, you will notice an abundance of mosses, ferns, and flowers growing on the inverted surface of the cliff face. Referred to as hanging gardens, these microclimates are a favorite of botanists. Among the lush green foliage of the maidenhair ferns, flowers such as the golden columbine, scarlet monkey flower, and shooting star sparkle.

Facing - Weeping Rock
Following - Hidden Canyon Trail Views

13) Temple of Sinawava & Riverside Walk

At end of the Zion Canyon Scenic Drive is the Temple of Sinawava, two stone towers standing as sentinels at the entrance hallway to the Narrows. The Riverside Walk begins at the shuttle stop, and after an easy, paved, one-mile stroll, it delivers you at the actual Gateway to the Narrows. Along the way, you also have the opportunity to enjoy several hanging gardens, and to spy one of Zion's most entertaining little birds, the American dipper.

Dippers are named for their strange behavior of constantly crouching up and down. Nobody knows for sure why they do this. When dippers aren't dipping, they are either flying above or below the surface of a stream. While submerged and hunting for aquatic invertebrates they are technically swimming, but the pattern of their wing beats is indistinguishable from the one they use to fly. You will be amazed how easily and quickly they can swim against the current.

Along the river, you may also see a potentially deadly beauty, the white, trumpet-shaped flowers of the poisonous sacred datura. The purple berries of the wild creeping holly grape are also best left to the wildlife. Flitting among the cottonwoods, maples, and ash, you may see grosbeaks, sparrows, and jays. From the river to the sky, the Riverside Walk is full of wildlife, if one is quiet and observant.

Top - Temple of Sinawava
Bottom - Riverside Walk

14) The Narrows

Where the pavement of the Riverside Walk ends, the Zion Narrows abruptly begins. The next step starts one of the most highly acclaimed adventures the National Park Service has to offer. However, it is not a step to be taken lightly. If you did not plan to continue before arriving at his point, you probably should not decide to do so now. There are three things few realize while standing in the hot sun, on a sandbar, in shin deep water at the end of the Riverside Walk:

First, the Narrows is a cold, dark place, where the sun only shines two to three hours each day.

Second, when the water is not chest deep, the riverbed is covered with slimy, slippery, softball-sized rocks. Footing could not be worse. Stumbling and bruises are common.

Third, a blue sky overhead does not mean that a thunderstorm beyond the horizon cannot turn the sparkling waters of the Virgin River into a bone-crushing torrent without warning.

What lies beyond the first bend is beauty and wonder like no other place on earth! Those that are best prepared will have the most enjoyable experience. Therefore, all who venture beyond the Gateway to the Narrows should wear shoes with good traction and strong ankle support, bring a walking stick or pole, check the weather forecast first, and allow for twice as much time as a hike of comparable distance.

One of the narrowest sections is less than a half-mile upstream. When the water flow is average, this is a chest-deep wade. When the water flow is high, it can be a neck-deep tiptoe or even a swim. At this point, the walls are less than 20 feet apart and soar nearly 1000 feet overhead. Only in the tributary known as Orderville Canyon do the walls come closer together. The Orderville Confluence is another mile and a half ahead. Keep in mind it takes most people another hour just to reach the confluence. Running out of time and daylight? Keep in mind you can always venture farther another day.

15) Kolob Canyons

These canyons are one of the best-kept secrets in all of Zion. This northern Kolob Canyon region of Zion boasts some of the most impressive and beautiful walls of rock in the entire park, and arguably, one of the best places for viewing sunsets in all of southern Utah.

Inside the Kolob Canyons Visitor Center, there is a small bookstore and an informative exhibit that explains how the famous Kolob Arch was formed. A scenic drive, paralleling the Hurricane Fault, extends from the visitor center. Along this fault, the rocks to the east have lurched upwards, a few feet at a time with each earthquake, until after 15 million years, they arrived at their current height. It has even offset relatively recent, geologically speaking, basaltic lava flows near the town of La Verkin. Now 4000 feet higher than where they began, the rock layers of the Kolob reveal 600 million years of earth history. When you round the corner and get your first look at the red walls and roads of the Kolob, you know why the expression "God's Country" applies here. Kolob is the name of the star in Mormon theology that is believed to be "closest to the throne of God."

The 5.4-mile moderate Taylor Creek Trail follows a small creek up past two historic cabins to Double Arch Alcove, which is an alcove topped with a blind arch. The 14-mile round trip hike to Kolob Arch begins at Lee Pass, named for John D. Lee, who hid in the Kolob Canyons for 20 years, eluding authorities after the 1857 Mountain Meadows Massacre, where he led a mob to ambush a California-bound wagon train, murdering all but the young children.

With each bend in the road, the panorama of the Kolob Canyons grows until it dominates the entire eastern horizon from north to south.

From the vantage of the Kolob Canyons Viewpoint and Timber Creek Overlooks, one can observe that Kolob is not one canyon, but several that merge to become Timber Creek. Some of the tributaries cut slot canyons obscured in their own shadows, while others, being hanging canyons, dump their contents over the edge of towering cliffs.

How long does it take these little creeks to carve so much grandeur? By using the relative age of lava flows, geologists have determined that the Virgin River was able to carve most of Zion Canyon in only 2 million years. Because the Kolob Canyons are farther away from the main channel of the Colorado River watershed, these must be even younger, perhaps only a million years?

Why are the Kolob cliffs so much redder than those of Zion Canyon? Geologists are undecided. Both are Navajo sandstone, composed of ancient sand dunes. The amount of iron in the rock determines the degree of redness. Some geologists feel that because the Zion Canyon rock has been eroding longer than the Kolob, the iron in the highest levels of the Zion Navajo sandstone has already leached out. Others suggest that since the Kolob rock was the western edge of the ancient desert, floods from mountains to the west mixed more iron in with these sand dunes. What do you think?

If you are like most people, Kolob will be the conclusion of your Zion experience. Absorb as much of the undefined energy of this national park as you can. Is it spiritual power? Scientific curiosity? Intoxicating beauty? Compelling history? Adventurous vibes? Or something else entirely? Perhaps there are no words that do it justice. But maybe, just maybe, we can all agree that the four letters: Z, I, O, N say enough.

16) Bryce Canyon

What does a Mormon ship-wright have in common with a wildlife menagerie nestled among enthralling geology adorned with a star-encrusted night sky? Answer: Bryce and the five years he was here. Welcome to Bryce Canyon National Park, named after shipwright Ebenezer Bryce. From the flame-colored spires beneath the rim, to the sparkling diamonds in the night sky, we hope you enjoy the magical beauty of Bryce Canyon.

Ebenezer Bryce was born in Dunblane, Scotland in 1830. As a shipwright's apprentice, he learned carpentry, the trade that would become his life. Bryce converted to the Church of Jesus Christ of Latter Day Saints and immigrated to the United States at the age of 17. Upon arriving in Utah, Bryce wed Mary Parker, and at the direction of the Mormon Church, the couple became serial homesteaders, going wherever the skills of a carpenter were most needed. They also managed to raise 12 children along the way! It was between 1875 and 1880 that the Bryces lived in the lower canyon. By logging the flanks and irrigating the floor of the canyon that his neighbors christened with his name, Ebenezer supplied the fledging community with wood and water. It is unclear to what extent Bryce appreciated the world wonder that would immortalize his name. His only enduring quote about this rock labyrinth expresses more pragmatism than awe: "It's a hell of place to lose a cow."

The beauty of Bryce Canyon was not lost upon J.W. Humphrey. Humphrey was the forest supervisor of lands that would eventually be united as the Dixie National Forest. Starting in 1916, he lobbied aggressively, sometimes even under an assumed name, to have the most scenic portion of his national forest bestowed with more protection than his agency could offer.

Step one occurred in 1923 when Bryce Canyon National Monu-ment was established under the administration of the U.S. Forest Ser-vice. The following year saw it renamed as Utah National Park and transferred to the National Park Ser-vice. In 1928, a significant boundary expansion restored the name to Bryce Canyon National Park.

The primary reason for es-tablishing the park was to protect and better understand the bizarre and beau-tiful geologic spires that would eventually be named "hoodoos", from the verb "hoodoo" meaning "to cast a spell". Later, as over-grazing, predator extermination, and pest poisoning took their toll on the surrounding region, Bryce also became a small but critical refuge for scores of animal species, including everything from the elusive mountain lion, to the highly endan-gered Utah prairie dog. Now, as the new and underestimated threat of light pollution spreads globally, Bryce Can-yon's park rangers use this last small sanctuary of natural darkness as a plat-form from which to champion the fragile beauty of the night sky.

Indeed, where Ebenezer Bryce was worried about losing his cows among the hoodoos, many now come to Bryce with the intent of get-ting a little lost themselves in its beauty. As Park Ranger Kevin Poe puts it, "There's no question that the rocks are enchanting, but it's also a hell of a place to lose yourself … among the stars."

17) Grand Canyon South Rim

Welcome to Grand Canyon National Park! As you approach the Grand Canyon, you are crossing the Colorado Plateau, a 130,000 square-mile bulge in the earth's surface spanning half of Utah and a good portion of Arizona, New Mexico, and Colorado. Around its edges are the upthrust Rocky Mountains, the stretched-apart Great Basin, the contorted rocks of Arizona's Transition Zone, and ancient volcanoes. Despite all the geologic activity around it, the plateau has managed to stay relatively flat and unfolded, but as a whole, it has been uplifted more than a mile.

It is the uplift, and the downcutting, that have created the canyon. About five to ten million years ago, the Colorado River began to carve its way down through the domed region on its way to the sea. Like a knife slicing through a layer cake, the mile-deep river canyon exposed multi-hued layers of time, a geologist's dream come true. However, you do not have to be a geologist to appreciate the canyon's grandeur.

Erosion by wind, water, and gravity not only widened the canyon; it created an amazing variety of towers and spires, ridges and side canyons, shadows and highlights. The rainbow of rock colors is most intense in early morning or late afternoon light. If you are lucky, you will see a storm chase through the canyon, casting shadows and mist as it goes.

Sightseers have been coming to view the wonders of the canyon since 1883. Prospectors soon found tourism more profitable than mining and built accommodations for them. One of the earliest visitors was Theodore Roosevelt, a lover of the West's wide-open spaces. He pushed for federal protection and in 1893, the area became a Forest Reserve. In 1908, it received a promotion to National Monument and in 1919, the National Park was formed. The most recent upgrade was in 1975, when its boundaries were expanded, doubling its size.

As you enter the park, you will receive a visitor's guide from the National Park Service, which is a great source of information on restaurants, lodging, parking, ranger talks, activities, and other guest services within or near the park. It includes maps, hours, prices and other timely and helpful information.

18) Grand Canyon North Rim

One of the most common questions in Arizona is "Which side of the Grand Canyon is better, the South Rim or North Rim?" Like most comparative debates, this one is best answered with "It depends … ". If cell coverage, IMAX theaters, warm temperatures, and proximity to interstates are a must, then the South Rim is for you. However, if you are looking to get away from the crowds and prefer conifers to cactus, the North Rim is your kind of paradise.

Getting to the North Rim is not easy. For most of the year, deep snow makes it inaccessible to all but the most athletic backcountry skiers. Even between late May and early October, the North Rim is fully three hours farther away from Las Vegas, Nevada or Phoenix, Arizona than the South Rim.

Perhaps it is the desert environment of the South Rim that makes the impression that the Grand Canyon is a calamity rather than a masterpiece. In the minds of the casual visitor, this South Rim perspective has always dominated. Looking up and across from the barren brink of the South Rim, classic descriptions like, "A gash in Nature's breast laid bare" seem accurate enough.

However, when looking down from the forested vantage of the North Rim, the Canyon's tremendous story of erosion looks less like devastation and more like craftsmanship.

Seeing the Grand Canyon as both a production and a destruction leads to a more enlightened understanding and appreciation of this world wonder. Indeed, just-a-big-hole-in-the-ground thinking is like accusing Michelangelo of defacing blocks of marble.

Theodore Roosevelt understood the canyon's duality. When proclaiming it a national monument in 1908, Roosevelt called it, "the most impressive piece of scenery I have ever looked at. It is beautiful and terrible and unearthly." Although Roosevelt spoke from the South Rim, if he were alive today, he would undoubtedly be a "north-rimmer". Speaking just as directly to untold future generations as he was the tourism developers in attendance, Roosevelt concluded his speech with a poignant caution, "Leave it as it is! You cannot improve upon it! The ages have been at work on it, and man can only mar it."

While a cynic, standing at the South Rim could grumble that Roosevelt's admonition was forgotten long ago, an optimist should take the cynic by the hand and say, "Roosevelt's Grand Canyon still exists! We just need to go to the North Rim." Welcome to the North Rim of Grand Canyon National Park!

North

WAYPOINT TOURS®

Zion Tour
Kolob Canyons Area

Gas station   Exit 42
To Cedar City,
Cedar Breaks National Monument,
and Salt Lake City   15

Horse Ranch Mountain
8726ft
2659m

Taylor   Creek
North   Fork

Taylor Creek Trail

Kolob Canyons Road
Exit 40

PARIA   Middle   Fork

Double Arch Alcove

Lee Pass Trailhead

South   Fork

Kolob Canyons Visitor Center
5074ft
1546m

15

Kolob Canyons Viewpoint

K O L O B

Nagunt Mesa
7785ft
2372m

La Verkin Creek Trail   Willis   Creek

Chasm Lake

Timber Creek Overlook Trail

C A N Y O N S

BEAR TRAP CANYON

8055ft
2455m

TIMBER   TOP   MOUNTAIN

Kolob Arch Trail

Langston Mountain
7408ft
2258m

Timber Creek

La Verkin Creek Trail

Kolob Arch

Gregory Butte
7705ft
2348m

Beatty Spring

LONG POINT

La Verkin   Creek

Hop Valley Trail

HOP   VALLEY

Burnt Mountain
7682ft
2341m

C   L   I   F   F   S

H   U   R   R   I   C   A   N   E

La Verkin   Creek

1) Zion*
2) Visitor Center
3) Pa'rus Trail
4) Watchman Trail*
5) Zion Museum
6) Zion-Mount Carmel Highway*
7) Canyon Overlook Trail*
8) Court of the Patriarchs
9) Zion Lodge
10) Emerald Pools Trails*
11) The Grotto & Angels Landing Trail*
12) Weeping Rock & Hidden Canyon Trails*
13) Temple of Sinawava & Riverside Walk*
14) The Narrows
15) Kolob Canyons*

Beyond this point, road not plowed in winter.

Firepit Knoll
7265ft
2214m

LOWER

Hop Valley Trailhead

Connector Trail

KOLOB

Spendlove Knoll
6895ft
2102m

LEE   VALLEY

SMITH

PLATEAU

Kolob Terrace Road

MESA

Tabernacle Dome
6430ft
1960m

Unpaved roads are impassable when wet.

Left Fork Trailhead

Zion Tour

THE NARROWS

West Rim Trail

North ↑

WAYPOINT TOURS©

ORDERVILLE CANYON

1) Zion*
2) Visitor Center
3) Pa'rus Trail
4) Watchman Trail*
5) Zion Museum
6) Zion-Mount Carmel Highway*
7) Canyon Overlook Trail*
8) Court of the Patriarchs
9) Zion Lodge
10) Emerald Pools Trails*
11) The Grotto & Angels Landing Trail*
12) Weeping Rock & Hidden Canyon Trails*
13) Temple of Sinawava & Riverside Walk*
14) The Narrows
15) Kolob Canyons*

Mountain of Mystery
6565ft
2001m

East Mesa Trail

Riverside Walk
14
Temple of Sinawava

Cabin Spring

7367ft
2245m

13

West Rim Trail

Weeping Rock

ECHO CANYON

12
Angels Landing

Hidden Canyon Trail

The Great White Throne
6744ft 2056m

HEAPS CANYON

11

10
Emerald Pools Trails

The Grotto

CANYON

9
Zion Lodge

COURT OF THE PATRIARCHS

8

ZION

Spring through fall, Zion Canyon Scenic Drive is open to shuttle buses only. Private vehicles are not allowed beyond Canyon Junction.

ZION NATIONAL PARK

TOWERS OF THE VIRGIN

The Sentinel
7157ft
2181m

Zion Canyon Scenic Drive

The East Temple
7709ft 2350m

1

Altar of Sacrifice
7505ft
2288m

Canyon Junction

Canyon Overlook Trail

Tunnel

Zion Human History Museum

The West Temple
7810ft
2380m

5

Parus Trail

6

Zion-Mount Carmel Highway

Tunnel
No bikes or pedestrians allowed. Ask about restrictions on large vehicles.

South Entrance

3

1

2

4
Watchman Trail

Zion Canyon Visitor Center

Springdale
3920ft
1195m

Mount Kinesava
7285ft
2220m

9

North Fork Virgin River

The Watchman 6545ft 1995m

www.waypointtours.com

Waypoint Tours®

Plan, Enhance & Cherish
Your Travel Adventures!

This Waypoint Tour® is your
personal tour guide unlocking the fas-
cinating highlights, history,
geology & nature of
Zion National Park.

Waypoint Tours® are entertaining,
educational, self-guided tours to help
plan your travel adventures,
enhance your travel experience &
cherish your travel memories.

Bryce Canyon
Grand Canyon
Grand Teton
San Francisco
Sedona Arizona
Yellowstone
Yosemite
Zion

Tour Books Plus DVD & MP3s
Tour Road Guides Plus CDs
Tour Guide Books

DVD & CD Complete Tour Packages
DVD Tour Guides
DVD Tour Postcards

Tour Solutions Plus More at
www.waypointtours.com
tours@waypointtours.com

Highlights, History, Geology,
Nature & More!

Credits

Book by Waypoint Tours
Editing by Laurie Ann
Photography by Waypoint Tours
Original Tour by Kevin Poe
Maps by the National Park Service
Bottom Bryce Photo by Ron Warner

Special thanks to the
Zion Natural History Association &
the Zion National Park Service.

Support Zion National Park
with a membership to the
Zion Natural History Association
Zion National Park
Springdale, Utah 84767
(800) 635-3959
www.zionpark.org

Zion National Park Service
Springdale, Utah 84767
(435) 772-3256
www.nps.gov/zion

Leave No Trace

WAYPOINT TOURS®

Optional Audio CD Contents

Audio CD Driving Tour (60 min)

Optional DVD-ROM Contents

DVD Narrated Tour (43 min)
MP3 Audio Tour (60 min)
PC Multimedia Screensaver
Digital Photo Gallery

Breathtaking Photography,
Professional Narration &
Beautiful Orchestration

DVD Plays Worldwide in
All Regions
Mastered in HDV in English
* Denotes Waypoints on DVD
PC Multimedia Screensaver &
Digital Photo Gallery Each Contain
70+ High-Resolution Photos

Professional Voicing by
Janet Ault & Mark Andrews
Recording by Audiomakers, Inc.
For private non-commercial use only
Detailed info & credits on DVD-ROM

Optional CD & DVD-ROM Info

Track #) Title

1) Zion*
2) Zion Canyon Visitor Center
3) Pa'rus Trail
4) Watchman Trail*
5) Zion Museum
6) Zion-Mount Carmel Highway*
7) Canyon Overlook Trail*
8) Court of the Patriarchs
9) Zion Lodge
10) Emerald Pools Trails*
11) The Grotto &
       Angels Landing Trail*
12) Hidden Canyon &
       Weeping Rock Trails*
13) Temple of Sinawava &
       Riverside Walk*
14) The Narrows
15) Kolob Canyons*

16) Bryce Canyon*
17) Grand Canyon*
18) Waypoint Tours*

Notes

www.ingramcontent.com/pod-product-compliance
Lightning Source LLC
Chambersburg PA
CBHW042107110426
42742CB00033BA/26